THE PERSIMMON IS AN EVENT

Mike Corrao is the author of numerous works including *Gut Text* (11:11 Press), *Under Reef* (Onomatopee), and *Smut-Maker* (Inside the Castle). His work often explores the haptic, architectural, and organismal, searching for ways to spatialize the text as a living object. As an artist and book designer, his work has been featured in the catalogs of Fonograf Editions, 11:11 Press, Apocalypse Party, Inside the Castle, and many more. As an editor, he operates CLOAK.wtf.

Also by Mike Corrao

-MANCER   *(Inside the Castle, 2022)*

Under Reef   *(Onomatopee, 2022)*

Cephalonegativity (w/ Evan Isoline)   *(Apocalypse Party, 2021)*

Desert Tiles   *(Equus, 2021)*

Rituals Performed in the Absence of Ganymede *(11:11 Press, 2021)*

SMUT-MAKER   *(Inside the Castle, 2020)*

Two Novels   *(Orson's Publishing, 2019)*

Gut Text   *(11:11 Press, 2019)*

Man, Oh Man   *(Orson's Publishing, 2018)*

The Persimmon is an Event

Mike Corrao

Broken Sleep Books

ISBN: 978-1-915760-46-3

Cover designed by Aaron Kent

Edited & Typeset by Aaron Kent

Broken Sleep Books Ltd
Rhydwen
Talgarreg
Ceredigion
SA44 4HB

Broken Sleep Books Ltd
Fair View
St Georges Road
Cornwall
PL26 7YH

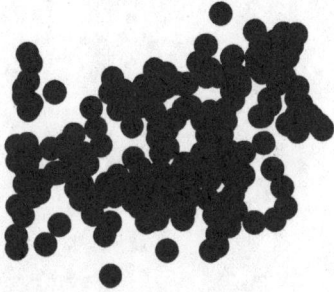

The Persimmon is an
Event

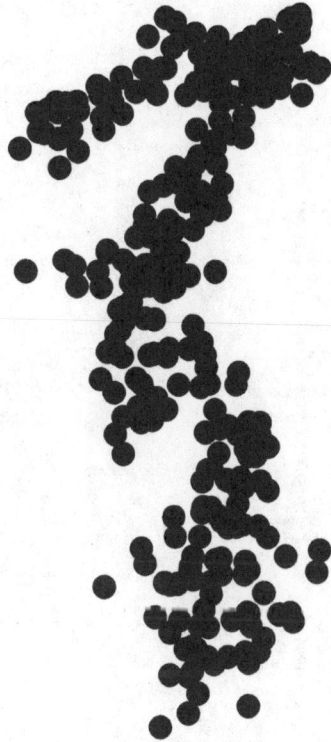

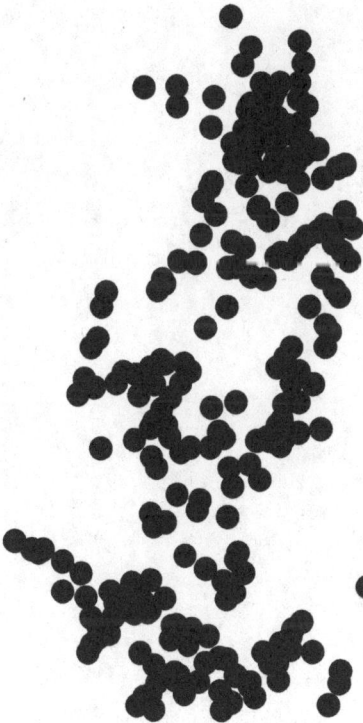

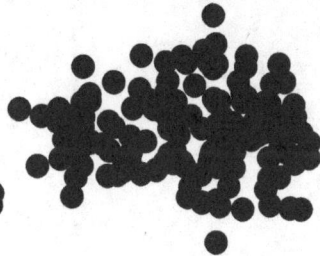

In this next scene, you are occupying something malleable. It is an object that can be molded the same as mud or clay.

/

We are standing completely still. This spot is deserted, and pitch-black.

/

Can you feel the flesh? It is not always meat. There are other materials. Equally fragile, sewn onto the skeletal frame just the same.

/

What do you wish to summon? What do you wish to see? We can't tune-in unless you want to.

Death is not death. It is a radical undoing of your position in space. The sudden or agonizingly slow changes of volume, mass, density.

/

You are not stuck. Your heart has the capacity to become a liver or a lung.

/

But it is time to construct the shrine. Burn the candles, dissect the persimmon, kiss the flesh, inside-out your open cuts, give your blood to the wound, the fruit's stone.

/

It illuminates in your throat and tightens in your stomach.

Can you see what's happening? In the pale glow. Under your translucent skin.

/

The ritual does what you've asked it to. It rearranges your body in a new shape.

/

Everything unravels.

/

Ecdysis draperies lay in loose coils. We examine your remains for medical / metaphysical / political reasons.

/

While your underbelly lays bare and tender. Your musculature begs to be liquified.

amorphous blob, gelatinous creature,   living stem.

/

Our anatomy can be traced back to a nodal point.

/

A blob is a transitional state of being. A blob is a malleable container
(Laura Hyunjhee Kim)

/

Slime is defined by its soft texture and decentralized anatomy.

/

It only moves when enough material has gathered that it is no
longer able to maintain its shape—when gravity has finally grated
away its will.

I cannot be untangled from my root-organism.

/

The *torso* is the irreducible node of the body. The birth and extension of new limbs. The rotund root into a levitating arbor.

/

There is nothing between us. The gateway stretches from anterior to posterior.

/

There is nothing between us. This is an open line of communication.

/

YOUR ONTOLOGY IS RADICAL IN ITS INSTABILITY. THE BODY DEMANDS METAMORPHOSIS.

You cannot expect to remain one way for long. You are cursed by potential.

/

This is a decadent arrangement of materials. As if we were sitting at a dining table. Or I at the table, and you on top of it. Suspended in gelatin.

/

It is okay if you vomit. I am vomiting right now. It's okay to vomit.

/

It is only you and I here.

Nymphs lounge in the open water while you give in to the onset of a new vessel / new self.

/

Ovid dances over a corpse—what used to be meat.

/

There is something wrong with my skin (Ursula Andkjær Olsen).

/

I desire to be unrecognizable. When I am cut open, it is not flesh that you see.

[DREAM] The shrine spawns luminous shadows whose features you cannot quite interpret. They mount your body and caress the edges of your open chest. Kissing the boundaries of the portal. Pressing their tongues on the *torso*'s labia and running their chins over the soft-tissue. They penetrate your center and submerge their sex in the red veil of the abyss.

/

This is the erotic morphological communique.

/

I won't be content until it's completely destroyed.

/

The *torso* is an abstract mechanism. In times of radical instability—the times that you now live in—it is subject to frequent and seemingly unpredictable changes.

When we return, you have become a wide wooden plate with metal stakes emerging from its surface.

/

This new anatomy renders your body a tool for ceremony / sacrifice.

/

You lure subjects onto your chest and embrace them. Letting their weight press onto the stakes until the flesh breaks and blood is pouring down each shaft onto the plate below.

/

You consume the flood and let it cake your interior.

/

You are a tool for creating corpses. For converting people into limp sacs.

Diagram of the new self (bed of stakes / an addiction to blood)

/

X IIIIIIIIIIII X IIIIIIIIIIIII X IIIIIIIIIIIII X IIIIIIIIIIIII X
X IIIIIIIIIIII X IIIIIIIIIIIII X IIIIIIIIIIIII X IIIIIIIIIIIII X
X IIIIIIIIIIII X IIIIIIIIIIIII X IIIIIIIIIIIII X IIIIIIIIIIIII X
X IIIIIIIIIIII X IIIIIIIIIIIII X IIIIIIIIIIIII X IIIIIIIIIIIII X
X IIIIIIIIIIII X IIIIIIIIIIIII X IIIIIIIIIIIII X IIIIIIIIIIIII X
X IIIIIIIIIIII X IIIIIIIIIIIII X IIIIIIIIIIIII X IIIIIIIIIIIII X
X IIIIIIIIIIII X IIIIIIIIIIIII X IIIIIIIIIIIII X IIIIIIIIIIIII X
X IIIIIIIIIIII X IIIIIIIIIIIII X IIIIIIIIIIIII X IIIIIIIIIIIII X
X IIIIIIIIIIII X IIIIIIIIIIIII X IIIIIIIIIIIII X IIIIIIIIIIIII X
X IIIIIIIIIIII X IIIIIIIIIIIII X IIIIIIIIIIIII X IIIIIIIIIIIII X
X IIIIIIIIIIII X IIIIIIIIIIIII X IIIIIIIIIIIII X IIIIIIIIIIIII X
X IIIIIIIIIIII X IIIIIIIIIIIII X IIIIIIIIIIIII X IIIIIIIIIIIII X
X IIIIIIIIIIII X IIIIIIIIIIIII X IIIIIIIIIIIII X IIIIIIIIIIIII X
X IIIIIIIIIIII X IIIIIIIIIIIII X IIIIIIIIIIIII X IIIIIIIIIIIII X

If it is weak, everything will peel away.

/

You'll be forced to reveal what's underneath.

/

I hope you know that we can't return to *the familiar* now.

/

An arcane procedure creates a wound that can't be healed. It is an unspoken agreement.

The *torso* (returning) is first depicted as a small bundle of redpink matter bound in a brace of ribs. An elaborate arrangement of organs is trying to escape.

/

ONE HUNDRED PHANTOM LIMBS PRESSING OUT OUT OUT OUT OUT

/

The arbor becomes a landmine. The arbor bends like witches in flight.

/

The ceremony of your undoing makes you nauseous.

/

We can't tune-in unless you want to.

The afterimage is a sultry darkness.

/

The skin of your forearms and calves smooth into bulbs of water. They sink into the floor and the walls—whatever you can press yourself against.

/

It is difficult to tell whether you are walking or hovering.

/

Every dreadful wound will heal eventually.

If we are quiet enough the vapors will cool and condense. They'll gather into a shape you feel more comfortable holding on to.

/

This is the height of fashion.

/

[ON PHANTOM LIMBS] The phantom limb is defined by its anti-corporeality. It is an ethereal entity. The silhouette of an arm. The outline of a leg. The *torso* absorbs its basest flesh until every pocket of air has been filled. If the phantom limb is an object of non-flesh, then we must assume that it is made of something else. That it is not subject to the radical transformations of death. You suffer a series of dreams that suggest that these entities are some kind of neural structure. That they are extensions of the unconscious growing beyond its physical constraints. You feel this same desire to move beyond your physical constraints.

Meanwhile, the onset of another transformation.

/

Condensation creates a node.

/

The root is suspended and flirting with blood. It appears in your dreams like a miracle or a portal to hell.

/

The node cannot speak. There is no mouth to tell us whether this *thing* is an object or subject.

It comes into being suddenly. Submerged in the apiary. Suspended in raw honey.

/

You fantasize about the pale and brittle structures forming in the semi-permiable spaces between the *torso* and the honey.

/

Through the gauntlet of bodily mutations, there is an inevitable mutation of desire as well.

/

The mirror creates a secondary image that overlaps and nearly replicates the original.

An oracular scene.

/

Your honeyed vessel slouches into the heat. Will you dance with me?

/

I feel the onset of anxiety. Everything is shivering and quiet.

/

And as quickly as you are conceived, you are diffused into a thin mist. There is sugar hovering in the air.

The desert flattens into a sheet of glass. You evaporate the desert into a void of particles.

/

What do you wish to summon? What do you wish to see?

/

The ozone layer swirls your body into a meteor of sugars.

/

What good is the persimmon?

/

Do you remember the iron maiden sleeping bag?

I am not interested in "devices." We are speaking through an arrangement of mirrors.

/

There is no direct connection between us. At least normally there isn't. I want to undo that if I can. Considering the circumstances.

/

Have you ever eaten a lemon on its own? Have you ever bitten into the skin and felt the oils fill your mouth?

/

Please don't let me fall apart.

The boundary shatters and you feel your consciousness descending.

/

The body is a topographical object.

/

We are traversing the width of your stomach.

/

Our focal point is the interaction. Between subjects, between subjects and their environment, between facets of the environment, between environments.

/

What is a "vice" ?

In
the
minefield
of
speech,

a murmuration

Your weight flattens across the width of the planet—becoming-gaia. The fractalizing *torso*.

/

Each appendage is a grain of sand. Moved by wind or will power.

/

I map out the passage from your stomach to your chest, following the exact procedures of a psychogeographic line.

/

My trajectory has already been determined. I am moving along the infinite, entering its canal as your shadow blocks the sun.

/

During my second passage, the lines have shifted. A and B are skewed by unknown variables.

A cartesian plane casts latticed shadows over the sand.

/

The wind uproots one thousand clastic limbs from your body.

/

You sense a displacement. It curves you into a new shape. It softens you into a set of interlocking rings.

/

COILING AND REPULSIVE.

/

Becoming meat once again   (an homage to meat)

The great ephemeral skin alludes to an anatomy that we are always outside of. The mobius strip curves through the esophagus, the intestines, the anus, and back without ever having reached an interior.

/

You are denied these pleasures of interiority. You are not welcome inside.

/

You lack a stable architecture. A building is not only walls. It is the floors and the ceilings as well. Every room that compartmentalizes the whole.

/

Unsew the quintessential facets of the body. Reduce the *torso* into its unwieldy matrices.

[NOTE] I am fixated on obliteration.
I am fixated on obliteration.
I am fixated on obliteration.
I am fixated on obliteration.
I am fixated on obliteration.
I am fixated on obliteration.
I am fixated on obliteration.
I am fixated on obliteration.
I am fixated on obliteration.
I am fixated on obliteration.

/

This is not death it is merely transformation.

/

We are crossing the subject-object divide.

/

Subject → Object → Supra-subject

The supra-subject exists above the subject. It is a human body projected horizontally with its palms pressed outwards.

/

There is no point in acting surprised.

/

What distance exists between you and I? Where we find ourselves now. Are you in front of me? Over my shoulder? Below me? I feel as if I could phase completely through you.

/

In this scene it has only been an hour.

You form a valley of flesh.

/

In the perineal region—the taint—with boundaries at the genitalia and anus.

/

The great ephemeral skin is localized as a liminal space of sexual desire and repulsion. I want you to run your finger along my taint. Please don't touch my taint.

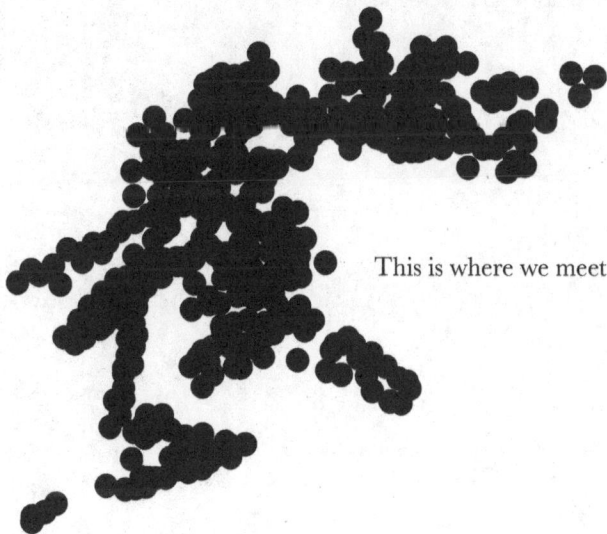

/

This is where we meet

Honey waxes the fur from your pores. Everything is cold. *Will you come on me?*

/

You do not know if this new shape is capable of dying. Your libido rises and you are unable to bear it any longer.

/

All of this *sloshing*

/

You perform a parthenogenetic conception at dusk, and extend your shadow across the landscape.

Another arrangement of lattices.

/

The sun hums against the skin of your back. Sweat rises from every pore. It feels as if you are gurgling moutfuls of pitch.

/

You think about how much you enjoyed having a mouth.

/

You worship the sun as if it is the reason for your transformations.

/

Meanwhile inside, an assemblage of clams.

You mimic the posture of a kratt, born from black currants and spare farm equipment.

/

You are given a task and thus life. It is difficult to remember when you were last capable of work.

/

Labor is a privilege of the kratt-body.

/

Without labor you become unstable. Whatever scythes and rakes have been strapped together to make your body begin to vibrate and loosen.

The kratt is valued as a golem. It is in the debt of whoever has forced life upon it.

/

I do not think that we are yet in a position to reach any conclusions. But I hope that by raising these concerns, we can begin the process of reaching them (REDACTED).

/

What turned it all to disgust? Is it the mask that I'm wearing?

/

Labor → Value → Depletion → Metamorphosis

In this kratt-body you are gifted 6,000 years of work. Plowing every field in the Estonian landscape until the ground has been eradicated and there is no more crop left to grow or harvest.

/

This leaves a contusion zone like a crater—the place where all of your effort has accumulated.

/

You can only care for so long before that care becomes harm, and that harm becomes an unconcealable scar.

/

If you hear a voice speaking to you from the base of your skull. It is not you. It is your ancient reptilian brain.

/

At the base of your skull, there is an unconceable scar.

→ adiposemelon
→ arboristthigh
→ contusionzone
→ antlerslouche

→ marimocarpet
→ pslamistgestaltkaput
→ persimmonsporekiss
→ krattscythelimb
→ algaeplumfeme

❶

Your relationship to the text is not as its equal, but as a lowly companion. In this study of Ovidian Dynamics, we see you taking up the position of a subject—that which is studied, surveyed, surveilled. The instabilities of the metamorphic process are something that you have awakened on your own, but this does not mean that we aren't allowed to watch.

I am the tome ! Dense with fat. Every page a *torso* with the desire to be severed / split open.

/

Will you still taste me? Drag your nail along my stomach. Reveal my innards and press them against your lips. Let the ink fill the crevices of your skin and dye your mouth black.

/

Is my ontology still legible to you?

/

Language carries itself across the width of my hips.

/

Jagged sentences are scrawled into the grooves of every rib. I want you to traverse each line, consume it, digest it.

This is the content of my creation. I am the sweet nectars of the persimmon.

/

There is a scar from where the fruit is picked from the tree, and stretch marks on the skin where you've grasped too tightly.

/

Persimmon → Metamorphosis   (Ovidian Scene)

/

The marimo-sun combs the landscape. Grating moss like hair through your teeth.

You still feel something at your center. The *torso*. The irreducible node.

⁄

This is where every change originates. Your intestines harden into petrified wood.

⁄

There is echoing in the canals of your digestive system.

When the wound opens, we can read each path the blood creates.

/

This is the return to meat (redpink). Even if it is not necessarily the body you started with.

/

Even if it not the body you ever wanted.

/

Wait here while everything is fragile. It will take a moment for the materials to fully congeal.

❶

It seems as if there nothing that cannot be mimicked. Your body is only limited by fragility and time.

→ selfmush

→ becomingsoweffigy

→ templefataltar

→ injuredreef

→ bodykaput

→ tubularorgan
→ flatskullkiss
→ foamclotpsalmist
→ doomtissue
→ interiormeadow

Ginger burns my tongue and in a fit of anger I uproot your stems from the soil.

/

If the *torso* is to be considered the nodal point of the arbor, what is its relationship to change? Can metamorphosis dissect the heart from the chest?

/

If this is to be the irreducible point, must it also be unmovable? Is it irreducible in its every quality, or only in its basest ontologies?

/

Can the arbor become a rhizome? Can the nodal point entangle itself in a web of identical nodes?

/

The origin of disruption. The *torso*. The right to spawning. The right to severing.

Land
across
the
ocean
of
the
dead

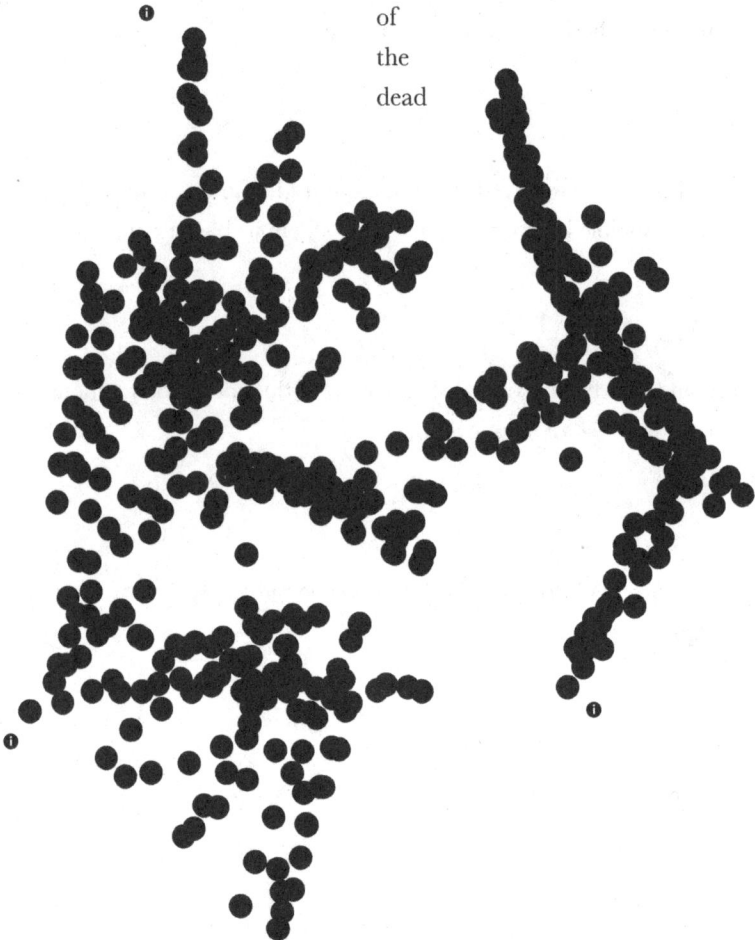

ⓘ

In the logic of the rhizomatic system—the network of identical nodes—each node must either be synchronized or be autonomous. If synchronized, then the act of metamorphosis is smooth and unified. The body unfolds as one into its new shape. If autonomous, then it is a miracle that we have not been rendered an akira of sloping flesh (dripping mound).

ⓘ

In the logic of the arborescent system, metamorphosis begins as the triggering of a single mechanism. This mechanism then triggers submissive mechanisms that surround it and commands them to undergo the same / complimentary transformations. The nodal point extends its influence over its outer appendages.

❶

We see early formations of the pathways that might convert the desert-body into a temple-body. If this is the case, then the suggestion of these results is that the traversable body is defined by the patterns of its traversal. Territorialization becomes a means for controlling and manipulating the metamorphic process, thus bringing us towards a more complete understanding of Ovidian Dynamics (although we are not brought to a better understanding of its initiating procedures i.e. the intimacy of the persimmon).

THE TEMPLE-BODY IS DEFINED BY ITS DIVINE POSTURE. IT IS NOT A MONUMENT MADE FROM STONE, BUT RATHER FROM FLESH AND FIBRE.

YOU BECOME A TOOL FOR WORSHIPING HALF-FORMED DIETIES / YET UNIMAGINED ORGANISMS.

The body as landscape (exterior) then becomes the body as construct (interior).

/

You become inhabitable. I want to take shelter inside of you.

/

I will enter from the whole you've cut through my abdomen that has now reflected back onto your own body.

/

You SPLIT and STRETCH.

/

In cases like these, I wear a veil over my face.

I will carve tissue from the buttresses of the ribcage, cut the pelvic floor into entryways, spread the ilium into a stage.

/

Your templed physique is bountiful. It welcomes my touch.

/

When the next sacrifice is performed, you feel no pain. You do not suffer. You simply watch, unappeased.

/

You are experiencing a constant influx of deterritorializations and reterritorializations.

A subject is removed of context, and made legible regardless of the absence of certain 'essential' nomenclatures.

/

The first metamorphosis is an exchange of labels.
Person → Slime

/

The second metamorphosis is an acceleration beyond the capacity of labels.

/

Each transformation demands the expansion of language. Not in the creation of new vocabularies, but in the complexifying of those already existing.

You expand inwards, shaping this lexicon as a schizopastoral landscape.

/

The performances of your mouth are strained as they attempt to utilize this endlessly augmented interior-language.

/

The definitions of pre-existing words mutate or disintegrate.

/

We are seeing a destruction of interpretable language. *Just listen to this, Mike* (Ed Atkins)

/

Meanwhile outside, a mammalian carcass evaporates.

At the moment of reterritorialization, a pocket is formed. The threshold expands.

/

The hesitation of your hands as you reach out to catch the grip of a falling body.

/

You allow your unconscious to guide you as a tarkovskyan lure towards desire. The ingress of the unknown terrain—dreamscape.

/

/

You wake up in the morning and you are tired. Because you have traversed an endless desert in your sleep.

The text asks you to do the same. It asks you to act out the labor of a reader.

/

You buy persimmons from the market and bring them back to your dwelling. You place them on the floor and cut them open with a soft knife. You kiss the flesh and this process begins.

/

Your body next resembles a clitoris.

/

Something (you) extends from the sheath, sliding out from between the labia and resting on the shelf of the mons pubis.

You are squirming and uncertain. You do not know if you are the serpent or the body beneath tensing at every touch.

/

It feels as if your stomach is going to fall out. You do not have a stomach. It feels as if every particle of air could kill you.

/

There is a wailing in the distance.

/

Metamorphosis occurs in the peripheries of your vision. Converting you from body → liquid.

The *torso* is a pool of fluid vibrating in the low frequencies of the guttural.

/

If we attempt to contextualize this new anatomy as another example of the schizopastoral practice, we might view the co-mingling of fluids as likened to a cacophony of voices.

/

Each droplet of blood / water / bile as one more vibration attempting utterance.

/

The schizopastoral dreams (landscape of mouths / landscape of complexification)

SLOP OF REDPINK KISSING THE SMOOTH LINOLEUM OF THE KITCHEN FLOOR.

/

Theoretical Framework → Foundational Texts

/

You crawl like a primordial ooze. Like the tar that encases long-dead organisms. Like the traumatized stare of a gorgon.

→ mocktissue
→ umbilicalseance
→ corpsicumfeme
→ gestaltlandibis

→ becomingentrail
→ exitwound
→ caesarianfume
→ interiorpsalm
→ chthonicmesh

The earth opens its maw and banishes you into the tartaran blackness of its core. Swallowing your fluid body.

/

At the coldest point — in the boundary between the heat of the sun and the heat of the mantle — you feel calm relief.

/

The hadean terrains of the planet's interior are never traversed with intention. Their discovery is always the result of an unexpected detour.

/

The *torso* approaches a threshold of amputation.

Your rooted body levitates over the open cave air. Flaunting its posture as a false sun. *Tear me open. Strip the skin.*

/

The hadean pastures are farmed by long-buried kratts. With rotted wood arms and rusting scythe hands.

/

Your body is split into two distinct sub-fractals.

/

You-derivative-one (yd1) and You-derivative-two (yd2) burrow into the wet soil.

> (The *torso* separated into its left and right halves.
> Where each begins to recreate its missing foil)

If the *torso* is the irreducible node, then what are the implications of its dissection?

/

What is inside of the thing that cannot be reduced?

/

Do you exist in a malleable fashion now? Are your appendages detachable?

/

When the scythe-hand of the kratt splits you in two, are you one thing that has been cut in half or are you two things that used to be one?

Can you be put back together?

/

If you are put back together will you be one thing or will you be
two fused together?

/

After 3000 years underground, yd1 and yd2 are reunited. They
suture their open wounds and create *you* once again.

/

We denote the point of severing.

- -

/

Orange residue.   Ginger-juices. Staining your skin.

Melons of adipose collect in the soil, cooling and congealing. Droplets harden into tissue and magnetize.

/

This gelatinous body is ready for its resurrection.

/

You plot your return into the atmosphere, even with the knowledge that this might be your undoing. That the sun might liquify you and your body might soak into the soil once again, until it has reached a depth of congelation and you are able to reform.

When you reach the surface you will see why the sun is worth worshiping.

/

Lift your hands to the sky and feel the rays of the solar-body as it imprints your flesh with the markings of maillard.

/

Reveal the oils of your skin. Reveal the sheen of your hairs.

/

Feel it all start to sizzle !

→ weightsloshslit

→ warmsoup

→ femekaput

→ funerarymesh

→ &what

→ mockproduce
→ pinkmousse
→ healingwound
→ cuttngthru
→ &what

DON'T YOU WANT TO SMELL THE BURNING? TO INSTIGATE ANOTHER
METAMORPHOSIS.

Ignite and become the new sun. Replace the archaic deity that came before you.

/

This body is made discernable by its markings. Certain runes / symbols hide underneath the surface.

/

[POST-OP] You move, I assume, with a certain rhythm. Patterns emerge from the aether, however complicated. How many variables do you contain? How long can they endure? In mapping the trajectory of your transformations, we begin assembling an understanding of Ovidian Dynamics—this budding field that we have found in the unknown expanse.

You are the first subject. And I am within you, studying each changing serif in the runes of your *torso*.

/

Splitting the persimmon, Kissing the flesh → The incipit action.

/

You are not you. You are you now.

/

You are you between forms and within forms. You are the slime, the bed of stakes, the blood, the sun, as much as you are the opening chest, the gathering pool.

There is an excruciating pain that floods your body. Remember, dismember.

/

It cannot be pleasant to feel your bones softening into phlegmish juices or to feel your blood hardening into fibrous roots.

/

You cannot cut me open. I am impenetrable.

- -

/

The sun presses the mat of its tongue over your back.

You fantasize about the detonation of your entire body. Not in some fever of annihilatory desires, but as a manifestation of your attraction to the great veil.

/

Specks of dust darken on the surface of your skin. Sprouting into chitinous webs—crawling across your body until your outermost layer has become hard and brittle.

/

Your interior retreats into the empty cavities of the shell. Liquifying (adapting to the shape of its container).

/

This new vessel is made in the likeness of the mollusc.

INT. Tentacles slither from every alcove. They crawl from the shell's entrance and press against the lip.

/

Recycle the liquified tissue of the molluscular-body !

/

Harden your intestines into beaks ! Stretch your heart and lungs into rope ! Soften your nail-beds into tender-flesh !

/

Your center is undetectable. Taking on the appearance of a nest or a mound.

You say, *I am the parody of a rhizome*. But you can only say this to yourself.

/

Reine Sprache → squid beak,   water siphon

/

The alien of liminal rites (tentacle-body)

/

You do not want to have a body if it means you will live alone.

The *torso* is a particle of sand floating through the interiors of this hellish configuration.

/

The process of Ovidian Dynamics, we might assume, is not driven by a set pattern.

/

The only certainty is that we will again become something new. We will continue to expand the interiority of this lexicon.

/

Press the orange of the persimmon into the crease of our lips. Pulverize every cell you touch.

In the metamorphic process, there must be some kind of anchor which holds the subject in place. That allows them to become something wholly new while still remaining themself (some amount of themself).

/

An anatomical object. Small and malleable.

/

Ovidian Dynamics is the study of the *torso* and its effects on the surrounding—supplementary—tissue.

/

She was bleeding. I didn't know. I didn't see anything (Chantal Akerman).

You feel the onset of your old body / the return of old-fashioned flesh.

/

You look as if you are concerned with rotation.

/

Mucin presses against the mantle and channels any remaining air out through the opening of the shell. The shell softens. The organs beneath multiply and rearrange.

/

This is a return to normalcy.

/

Your hips emerge from the lower vertebrae of the spine. Cords of fluid flex and bend. *This is what it means to be alive.*

You feel human again. Even if you are not. Even though you are still unidentifiable. Skin macerated under writhing tissue.

/

Ugliness is a kind of death.

/

Can you see my complexion in the sight picture?

/

Your head begins to form, with mouth and nostrils emerging first from the bulging mass of the neck.

INT. Complex proteins instruct undesignated tissue to become delicate and hollow. Your eyes emerge from slits cut above the nostrils. Bone and muscle gather at the shoulders, then the hips.

/

As the first limbs begin to take shape, the surrounding web of tentacles migrate inward. They caress the skin and coil above each orifice.

/

You feel yourself condensing into one organism.

/

Every tentacle invades your body.

We can't tune-in unless you want to.

/

[POST OP] Flooding your abdomen, suffocating your mouth, expanding your nostrils, engulfing your eyes. You feel as if all of the air has been expelled from your body. Replaced with gelatin and water.

/

You accept these changes and swallow the fluid discharge of each antiquated flare.

The Torso:

It is okay to be everything at once.

/

At its root, minimalism is a desire to disappear.

/

It is the removal of every object attached to your identity (from loose associations to intimate connections), until there is nothing left.

/

It is an ontology against objects.

The ascetic desire to prove that you can be animate without kindness to the inanimate.

/

Meanwhile outside, there is an experimental gestalt burning in the yard.

/

This is the result of a cataclysmic consumption.

/

The body has become a false icon. You consider destroying it, but you realize that the two of you have now become inseparable.

/

An unattainable subjecthood   objet petit b.

You forget the intricacies that come with exterior language. You can only remember the ways in which your body has been communicating with itself.

/

It is not healthy to hide inside of other people.

/

In the digital landscape of the 2020s.

/

An orphic figure—nymph or mourner—asks that the frayed hairs in your monitor be turned into lyre strings.

Will you play me a hymn?

/

Will you play me a severing   note?

/

The interior zones of the body don't have to be exclusively physical.

/

Corporeality alludes to the *reality* of the body. Not just to its participation in the natural world.

/

It is often the case that the corporeal drifts into unnatural places.

You are in the distance somewhere, watching as this vessel begins to mutate.

/

The *torso* is a speck of dust hovering in the void.

/

IN THE DISTANCE   *AN EXPANDED FIELD*

/

It is not healthy to hide inside of other people.

THE SIMULACRUM IS A TEMPORARY STATE. YOUR HERETICAL THRONE IS DISMANTLED AND YOU ARE IN YOUR BODY ONCE AGAIN. NOW, AS IT HAS BEGUN TO MELT.

This is a prophetic machine. Illuminated by the light of your eyes.

/

It is a simulation of every change yet to come. Each step that must be taken to remove the veil that obfuscates your intentions.

/

The mass of veins screaming.

/

The rhizome unfurls into a peacocked web and liquifies. It burns through the outermost layers of your skin. Turning the flesh beigepink and irritable.

/

You're melting, baby !

Slime and syrup pour from your mouth. Pooling on the ground beneath you—hunched and coughing.

/

Clinging their tendrils onto each nail digging into the floor. Then, climbing over your digits, onto the backs of your hands, up your wrist.

/

You cannot stop vomiting. This is what it means to be alive. You feel as if you are suffocating on your own body.

/

We reward your raw throat / burning esophagus with a half-formed ecosystem.

Microbes crawl along you forearms and thighs.

/

They pluck the hairs from your skin and burrow into your pores. They turn your blood viscous, infecting each vein with jets of slime, flickering their tongues against the open slit.

/

They inhabit you as if you are a new planet. Microlithic gaia lying fetal in an undisclosed cave.

/

What intimate rituals will you attempt to perform next?

Out of the earth you grow three heads. Each with long snouts and rows of sharpened teeth.

/

What kind of hound guards the gates of the underworld? Does it live on dry land? Or does it wade knee-deep in the river.

/

Tufts of hair emerge from the spine. Coarse and gray.

/

Your flesh is coated in warmth. The microbes enjoy a radiant heat.

/

The forest of time is vast and hung with bodies.

Cerberus → Field of anuses

/

Do you know what kind of entity exists beyond the gate / gait?

/

I am the witness of every fatality. (Pluto)

/

Each death is performed with the assumption that it will not happen again—we have arrived at the end of production.

/

An existent subject is made from non-existent objects.

There is no outline surrounding your body.

- -

╱

I take shape only so that I might fall apart again.

╱

I want to drag my body into the blurred landscape.

╱

You pace back and forth under the heat of the hell-fire.

❶

This ontological shift from organismal to mythological denotes the potentiality of a more complex sub-set of metamorphic variables. Inferring that you are able to assume the context surrounding a completely separate entity and inhabit its history.

The text surrounding you is developed through a mix of sorcery and academic research.

/

Will you be my foul boatman?

/

In the position of the Cerberus, you feel a desire to consume.

/

You feel the desires of beheading.

/

Every limb is dynamically rendered. This simulacrum laughs as you test the cords holding each skull upright.

The arbor is a fertile *torso* with the capacity to grow new sub-*torso*s (appendages).

/

The rhizome is a sterile *torso* only capable of expanding / fractalizing what is already present.

/

Are you a network of arms or ribs?

/

What do you wish to summon? What do you wish to see?

The necropastoral is a zone of distinctly earthly monuments. It is rife with insects and moss.

/

You take on the appearance of a beautiful fungus.

/

Your head is hovering above the soil, but your *torso* is buried underneath.

/

INT. Your organs grow long and thin. They gather at the exits—mouth, anus, ears, genitalia.

/

EXT. Your organs crawl out from their dwellings and burrow into the cool soil.

When there is nothing left inside of you, the remaining cavity collapses and assimilates.

/

Web of Innards. Network of Nerves.

/

I am a neural structure.

/

There is no dry land remaining. Your skin prunes. It becomes fragile and tearable.

Drawing blood from an unknown planet. (Ж)

——— ———————————— ——————— ——————————

/

The (Ж) is a theatre of poorly rendered polygons. Its name represents something that cannot be reconstructed by language.

/

Do you know what you are looking at? It is a product of well-trained machines.

/

The (Ж) is a primordial originator. It fuels the metamorphic process.

/

Now that your body has expended all of its own energy.

Traitor !   Robber !

/

You are mad but you do not know why.

/

Maybe you expected more from me—us. After all of the transformations you've suffered, why break down now?

/

Six feet beneath the flesh.

/.

The sun ignites. (Ж) curls into a husk. You feel its blood flowing through you.

Why do you create this prison for yourself? The right to alien-ness consumes.

/

You perform intricate choreographies on the surface of the dying (Ж). Its textures react to your touch. The flat-images of each face distort upon contact.

/

Hollow furnaces on fire.

/

What does a digital object look like? When you hold it in your hand?

/

(Ж) liquifies in your veins—tubular organs / segments of the greater root.

You hope that this will catalyze a return to meat.

/

A series of dreams tells you that your actions will not go unnoticed. Whatever deity summons these transformations watches from above / outside / beyond.

/

Ovid. Narcissus. Post-Narcissus. Ganymede. Hermaphrodite.

/

What do you wish to summon? What do you wish to see?

/

I evoke the muses. Like a dog barking at the television.

When the rhizome congeals into one body—the *torso* in its most humanoid form—you will lift your hands to Mars and weep.

/

The persimmon is a tool for taking your body apart. At the ritual's incipit, you doubted the effectiveness of this tool.

/

Ambient vibrations create micro-tears across your musculoskeletal system.

/

For the first time, you notice a pattern in your transformations—not in the predictability of each new anatomy, but in this inevitable return to meat.

/

The return to meat is a time for rest.

You close your eyes and imagine a vast dinner laid out on the table in front of you.

(Stewed root vegetables, calasparra rice, pickled king trumpets, charred gem lettuce, roasted heirloom tomatoes, raw and mashed garlic, sheets of nori, vinaigrette stirred from olive oil and lemon juice, halved avocados, candied almonds, pureed peas, jicama and kumquats, prosciutto-slices of grapefruit, basmati rice, beet marmalade spread over toast, gnocchi, harissa olives, blackberry scones and sweet potato danishes, pickled pearl onions, moon grapes, cremini mushrooms stirred through white wine sauce, carrot ginger salads, roasted walnuts and macadamias, miso soup and blistered shiitake, bruschetta, fried capers, scorched cauliflower, thin slices of kohlrabi, pickled watermelon rind, fresh soft cooked eggs, artichoke hearts and roasted brussel sprouts, bushels of beet stalk, roasted carrots, minestrone and faro, serrano peppers, swiss chard, celery root, radicchio, lemon veloute over orecchiette, sundried tomato pesto, broccoli puree, sour melon, pickled crab apples, chimichurri, focaccia, herb gremolata, dashi, spring onions, spoonfuls of honey, blood oranges, peaches stewed in syrup, quartered nectarines, caramelized lemons, roasted figs, charred cabbage, enoki broth, honeycrisp apples, golden beets in brown butter, bread pudding, coffee cake, roasted butternut squash, clementines and plums, pumpkin bisque, and pickled pears)

None of this is real.

/

But you are pleased that it could be. That you could hold each plate in your hands and taste each flavor on your tongue.

/

Strata crumble in the exposed flesh between your bones.

/

You are a network of caves. Your arms extend and split. Proto-limbs branch from mutated digits. Your legs curl around your *torso*.

/

This is the slow dance of xibalba.

It is difficult to explain where we are standing now, still in front of the audience (still disguised as something 'cinematic' if we can say so without vomiting).

/

The *torso* becomes a large chamber illuminated by torches.

/

Architecture is not about the moment of completion, but about the totality of time and space extending throughout the process of design, construction, completion, and utilization. (Ito).

/

You continue your descent. Unfettered by the growing nausea and disorientation.

The cave expands into an intricate labyrinth. You do not know what you look like. Still you feel every new limb as it weaves into more and more complex knots.

/

Right to concavity / hole-ness

/

Ovidian Dynamics is a study of localized ecologies.

/

Biomes are disassembled. Research is performed. The façade is perpetuated.

/

Our intention is to understand ourself.

Your metamorphosis—ad nauseum—is capable of manufacturing / repurposing mythological information.

/

Digital reconstructions of Jupiter (અ)

An altar appears in the central chamber of your cave-body.

/

Where are you hiding?

We only have a loose understanding of liminal deities. Even as the participants arrive.

/

Hekate is gifted a black dog and a small modicum of blood.

/

Traces of (Ж) remain in your body for 20,000,000 years.

/

Something manifests in the gut.

/

Mineralized serpents excavate sandstone aquifers hidden deep within the crust.

/

Each serpent is a tool for creating empty space. Tubular cavities mimicking the functions of a base-*torso*.

(આ) represents the effort in your transgressions.

/

Static liquifies in the dense walls between each route.

/

Your mouth is filled with syrup and sand. It tears at your gums and scores your enamel.

/

Cave System → Intestinal Tract

/

What does it feel like? To expand the width of the earth. And burrow into her soil.

Primitive brass instruments blare in cacophonous arrhythmia.

/

What do you wish to summon? What do you wish to see?

/

The deafening yawn of (외) as he feels the curves of your cave-body. Saying something about wet soil and scorched earth.

/

Right to erotic-ness

/

When (외) approaches and presses his body against you and kisses the insides of your thighs, you do not know what he will expect of you, or if you are entirely interested.

But your body is too expansive. It slithers through the shallow crust of the planet.

/

You summon the veins of the Earth. You give birth to its pulmonary system. Letting fluid flow through you.

/

(अ) cannot find the width of your body. He cannot find head or orifice.

/

You fantasize your sex mutating in the shape of an arbor. You fantasize (अ) finding the branches of your tree-body and pressing his tongue against their point.

INT. Pink hues of light. Running water.

⁄

(왈) departs. He says that he will come back when your body is less beautiful.

⁄

And you wait.

⁄

Letting the earth use you—You take this time to rest. Cool water flows through your belly and calms your nerves.

You fuel the slow growing organisms of the surface.

/

Fungus, moss-film, meadows, rodents, and insects

/

Everyone does their best to forget you.

/

We operate on bug time.

/

Eventually you will grow too large and the emptiness of your insides will no longer be able to sustain the crust above.

You anticipate an inevitable return to the sun.

/

Cave-body → Ruined desert

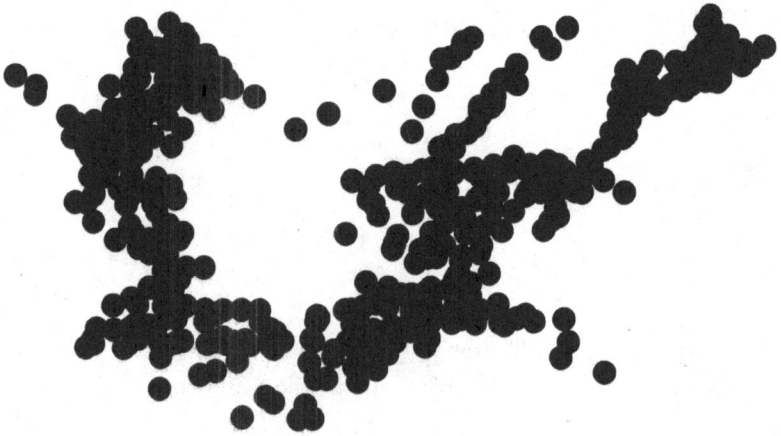

/

/

Sifting landmines from buckets of sand.

Maybe it is important that such feelings remain unconveyable.

/

After 0000000000000000 years, the erotics of this vessel become unsustainable. The labyrinth destroys itself.

/

Your sandstone body crumbles into dust.

/

You become small and delicate as the metamorphic process begins once again.

EXT. The sun illuminates your every particle and you bask in the heat of its radiation.

/

Pitch oozes from the remaining walls of the cave system. It coagulates in the pores of the sandstone and stains the exposed veins.

/

Dust and dirt collect in trail. Marching caravans.

/

[DREAMSCAPE] You cup your hands against the wall and let the pitch run down your fingers. When you cannot hold any more you bring it to your lips and consume it. You relax your throat as it crawls down your esophagus.

All of the fluids of your body are replaced with pitch.

/

When you weep it coagulates in your tear ducts and stains your face. It oozes from your open cuts and suffocates your tongue

/

Ovidian Dynamics is an examination of the self as its limits become unclassifiable.

/

With each new anatomy you are forced to reacclimate to your body—to overcome intense feelings dysmorphia.

The return to meat is a moment of solace. But its arrival is always unpredictable.

/

You are tar pits. You are welling droplets of pitch.

/

Mineral-to-living. Extinction-fluid

/

Slabs of unmined salt fall like glaciers. Collapsing into dust and smoke. Coating your soft flesh in blisters.

/

The water hisses from your body. It collects on the surface atop a newly-formed skin.

Pitch-Sentience.   Becoming-Subject.

/

There is comfort in this return to the slime-esque. You are once
again a primordial ooze.

/

... this spasming, chemically induced, methed-up, mutating Death time...
(Joyelle McSweeney)

/

The scope of your chronology has changed. Time expands and
contracts with each new vessel.
                           (Accelerating as ginger or fat, and
                           slowing to near stillness as slime
                           or desert)

The pitch-body is an eternal witness, seeing all that is and has been. It expands across time.

/

It is defined by the time-image. By the atemporal segments that make up its temporal being.

/

Pitch crawls over the surface of the porous sandstone, latching its tendrils onto each jut and edge.

/

You feel your self vibrating violently beneath the surface.

→ terrorpig
→ meteorfluid
→ cropyield
→ persimmonselfkaput
→ psalmfeme

→ nullscene
→ deathmatch
→ mossfilm

❶

You move inwards—inhabiting an abyssopelagic zone hidden within your psyche. You conduct experiments, testing the instabilities of this vessel. Extracting samples and testing them in an astral laboratory. Your research reveals nothing.

An overwhelming fatigue infects your body.

/

You experience a tarkovskyan dilation of time and space. Where everything is slow and dream-like. Each moment of extreme speed obscured from view.

/

Dream Conductivity → Bug Time

/

You fantasize your navigation of an anomalous zone. Throwing knots of cloth from one patch of grass to the next.

EXT. The remaining cave walls begin to collapse. The sun reveals itself. Boiling the earth.

/

You prepare for hibernation. You attempt to rest before the inevitable onset of your next transformation.

/

Right to sleep / dormancy

/

Without origin, a third-party entity learns of what's happening and assembles something they've named the *Ovidian Research Group*.

They isolate the halved persimmon and prob it with robotic instruments. They extract samples and test the fruit's firmness.

/

"The persimmon is a catalyst for psycho-biological reactions–most of which are unpredictable." (REDACTED)

/

There is always a return to meat.

/

The *Ovidian Research Group* prepares for your next return by constructing 'protective suits' and 'stablizing equipment'.

They engineer an exoskeleton with the intention of quickly attaching it to your body the moment it becomes recognizable.

/

You don't like that they are thinking of you now as an object, as something non-human.

/

The masks above the stage have been replaced with an ox-head and horse-face.

/

Mucous accumulates around the entrances of your body.

The threshold of subject and object is made traversable once again. You summon a portal into meatspace.

/

When you arrive, there are three quarantined figures here waiting for you. One of them is holding a heap of rare earth metals.

/

Before you can emit a sound (before you can learn if you've regained the ability to speak), the two remaining figures grab you and hold you down.

/

They wait for the *torso* to fully surface.

/

The third frantically straps the skeletonized tangle around your waist and shoulders.

It doesn't feel right to be held like this.

/

There is a large bruise forming on your back. It is purple and brown.

/

Microlithic gaia congealing.

/

You are rendered irreducible. The *torso* levitating over fire. Without limb or head. Coiled in new adornments.

/

Witches flight → the unmetamorphized frame

Torso configuration:

The skeletal metals are vibrating around your upset body.

/

Your hips and shoulders curve in on themselves. They attempt to remove evidence of your previous limbs.

/

The *torso* is an immobile object. It is only made to look human.

/

The *Ovidian Research Group* is not concerned with your well-being. They are only interested in slowing your body down.

They don't want you to accelerate forward—to become something beautiful and undefinable.

/

The ribs are a cage that confines the interior and maintains the façade.

/

You are more than basic viscera. You are a fractal of bodily potentials.

/

[NOTE]   The *Ovidian Research Group* emit an ambient static that engulfs your ears. You hear it in your jaw—a phantom pain—and it reverberates into your throat.

Don't you want to know what's under those plastic suits?

- -

/

You do not want to be reduced to an object.

/

You are beyond object. You are beyond subject.

/

The *torso* is an irreducible node. You are beyond the patronizing
formulas that they have created to confine you.

The body becomes a language of annihilation. Destroying the already fragile specificity of utterance.

/

Ovid mocks your anchored pre-corpse.

/

The exoskeleton is a means of confining you to one mode. But you are capable of much more.

/

Right to instability / change

/

The sun envies you. As it bakes your skin and fantasizes of your effigy-death.

In this simplified vessel you have been rendered an artifact.

/

Your teeth embedded in the flesh of the persimmon.

/

Can you see what they have given you? Through all of this discomfort there is progress. You are more vast than you ever could have been without their help.

/

The persimmon is a catalyst. Your kiss is the beginning of your reaction / co-mingling.

/

Ovidian Dynamics is a study of your intimate relations with fruit.

Persimmon → Self-actualization

/

The quarantined figures drag your *torso* onto a wood altar—made haphazardly while their focus was drawn elsewhere.

/

You rest at its center, anchored by splinters.

/

The *torso*'s status as artifact is superficial. It is only another step through the metamorphic process.

/

You fantasize the destruction of this exoskeleton. You do not like living without a head.

The *torso* is an anatomical object, meaning that it can be killed—
whatever that entails.

/

Death is not death. It is a radical undoing of your position in
space.

/

The quarantined figures probe various parts of your body. They
draw blood samples and remove grafts of skin, soft tissue.

/

They place these samples under microscopes and inside various
blinking machines.

INT. Your organs remain still. They rest in the fluids of your body. Submerged, complacent.

/

A ring of halved persimmons surround you. Delicately placed on the wood altar.

/

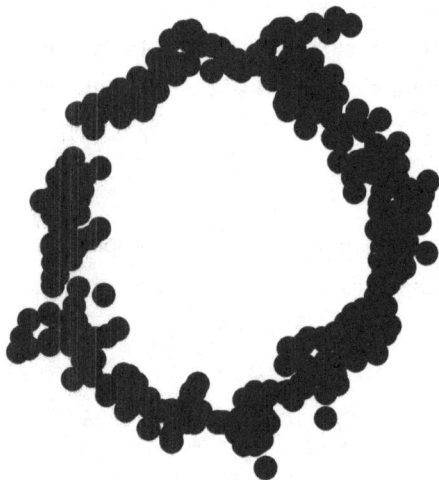

You feel as if you are being mocked.

/

The exoskeleton grasp your spine. They flaunt the fact that you cannot escape.

/

But you do not listen. You attempt to displace yourself. To expand your *torso* beyond the limitations of the configurations.

/

You refuse this status as object. You do not want to be studied by these sterile fucks.

You demand self-examination. Ovidian Dynamics is a study of the self.

/

You convert your organs into a labyrinth of stone and mucous.

/

You create a demonology of the anatomical form. Summoning the catalyst of your metamorphosis. Begging that you be made into something undefinable.

/

Right to expansion / Interiority + Exteriority

You feel excruciating pain as stone tendrils penetrate your skin, slithering through your abdomen and into the open air.

/

They latch onto the skeletal frame and pull it apart.

/

Mucous seeps from your open wounds.

/

The quarantined figures attempt to reassemble the configuration but there is nothing that can be done.

You grow. Your stone tendrils probe the wood altar, the open room, the persimmons. They map the environment and imprint its layout in your mind.

/

You see without seeing.

/

Localized topologies vibrate through your bones.

/

(Ж) moans as you give birth to a new head.

You summon a skull and gray matter from the stump of your neck.

/

You accelerate towards metamorphosis. Drawing wood dust and tar over the exposed flesh.

/

The stone tendrils lift you from the altar.

/

Splinters burrow around the base of your half-formed femurs.

/

They mutate into antennae and further map your surroundings— primitive eyes begin to form.

The persimmons hum a unified song.

/

When you are levitating above the wood altar, you let the tendrils sever from your body.

/

The *torso* moans arrhythmic noise into the abyss.

/

What do you wish to summon? What do you wish to see?

/

Ovidian Dynamics is a study of dysmorphia and its eventual subversion.

Meaning of   the removal of anchors.

                              /

The supra-subject emerging from its chthonic hiatus.

                              /

Now we will start talking (M Kitchell).

                              /

Your body engulfs the sun. You displace the object of worship.

Made with great thanks to Logan Berry, Daymian Snowden, and Steve Barbaro.

LAY OUT YOUR UNREST

www.ingramcontent.com/pod-product-compliance
Lightning Source LLC
LaVergne TN
LVHW030054090426
835513LV00034B/2401